Good to Great ...in 30 minutes

THE EXPERT GUIDE TO **JIM COLLINS'S**

Good
to Great
...in 30 minutes

THE 30 MINUTE EXPERT SERIES

GARAMOND
—— PRESS ——

Contents

At a Glance

This book is an extended review of *Good to Great: Why Some Companies Make the Leap... and Others Don't,* by Jim Collins. In *Good to Great,* Collins plays on an old adage—"the perfect is the enemy of the good"—and shows how the good becomes the enemy of the great in business organizations. Collins says companies that have made what he calls "the leap from good to great" are those that have learned to transcend the "curse of competence" by shifting their focus away from what they're already good at doing and concentrating instead on what they have the potential to do better than any other company.

The review begins with a brief introduction to *Good to Great.* Next comes a section that includes information about the book and the author, a summary of readers' responses to the book—the good and the not so good, from professional reviewers as well as from bloggers and other interested readers—and a synopsis of *Good to Great.* That section is followed by a detailed discussion of the book's key concepts. Finally, the main points of this review are briefly restated, in a way that may well inspire you to get your own copy of Jim Collins's book and see for yourself why *Good to Great* is such a favorite with readers. Also included are a list of key terms used in *Good to Great* and recommendations for further reading.

Understanding
Good to Great

ABOUT THE BOOK

Jim Collins got the idea for writing *Good to Great* when a guest at a dinner party told him that his previous book, *Built to Last,* had little to offer companies that were trying to make the jump from moderate success to stellar performance, since *Built to Last* explored the ways and means of companies that had begun with and then maintained an iconic level of achievement. Thus *Good to Great* evolved as a kind of prequel to *Built to Last,* as Collins decided to explore the question of whether a company that was performing well could surpass merely good performance and break out to greatness.

Collins put together a research team of twenty-one members, and for the next five years he and his colleagues examined scores of companies on the Fortune 500 list. They eventually chose eleven companies that fit their criteria: Each company had to have shown "good" performance, defined as having its stock outperform the market by a factor of 1.25 for at least fifteen years before a transition point, after which the company had to have shown "great" performance, defined as having its stock outperform the market by a factor of 3 for at least fifteen more years. They also looked at companies that had tried but failed to make the "greatness" grade.

Armed with reams of data, information culled from interviews with CEOs and other leaders, and the fruit of many team discussions and debates about what all the data meant, Collins discovered that all the good-to-great companies had certain attributes in common, and that companies falling short of greatness lacked one or more of these attributes.

Upon its publication in 2001, *Good to Great* was immediately hailed as a radical road map to stellar success, and its followers were legion. More than four million copies were sold, and it became one of the best-selling management books of all time.

ABOUT THE AUTHOR

Jim Collins was born in 1958 in Boulder, Colorado. He earned degrees in business administration and mathematical science from Stanford University before beginning his teaching and research career at Stanford's Graduate School of Business. In 1995 he returned to Boulder, where he founded his management research laboratory and now lives with his wife, Joanne Ernst.

At the laboratory, Collins and his five core employees, sometimes assisted by student researchers, examine questions that interest them in the areas of business practices and strategies. After compiling as much information as they can from a variety of sources, they begin the process of debating the conclusions they've drawn from their collective immersion in this material. Collins then uses this information and the group's insights to write his books, which include not just *Good to Great* but also *Built to Last: Successful Habits of Visionary Companies* (1994), coauthored with Jerry I. Porras; *How the Mighty Fall: And Why Some Companies Never Give In* (2009); and his most recent work, *Great by Choice: Uncertainty, Chaos, and Luck—Why Some Thrive Despite Them All* (2011), coauthored with Morten T. Hansen and examining the unstable business and social environment for companies today.

CRITICAL RECEPTION

The Upside

As already noted, Jim Collins's *Good to Great* has sold over four million copies since 2001, and more than a dozen years later the book is still available in hardcover. Those are two indisputable signs of its positive reception.

The book has avid followers in the business world, of course. For instance, the website of the British-based IT/organizational consulting company Agilier praises *Good to Great* as "tremendous" and "thoroughly researched," and William J. Hass, writing for the website of the Turnaround Management Association, notes Collins's "great metaphors" and describes the book's "rich" stories and concepts as "a welcome addition to any turnaround practitioner's tool bag." (Hass's endorsement does, however, come with a caveat about the book's "limitations," in the form of research that suffers from selection bias as well as from overdependence on secondary sources.)

But "the key to the book's popularity lies elsewhere" than in the world of CEOs and entrepreneurs, according to Kevin Maney of *USA Today*, who says HarperBusiness, the book's publisher, estimates that readers outside the corporate world—ministers, police chiefs, school principals, people who run homeless shelters, orchestra leaders, and coaches in a variety of professional and amateur sports—now comprise at least 50 percent of the book's paying audience because the book's "findings and lessons are universal."

To take just one example of the book's wide appeal, when Mike Bonem, an organizational consultant, first worked with churches on issues of pastoral leadership, he "knew the tendency of many churches to make excuses rather than confront underperforming staff members," he says. With *Good to Great*'s staffing metaphor of getting "the right people on the bus (and the wrong people off the bus)" in mind, he asked himself, "Wouldn't the church be much more effective for the Kingdom if we got the wrong people off the bus?"

Another example of *Good to Great*'s broad popularity comes from Jeff Janssen of the Janssen Sports Leadership Center in Cary, North Carolina. On the website of the Championship Coaches Network, Janssen outlines how the major principles laid out in the book can be applied to the world of sports and coaching.

Schools, too, have benefited from the *Good to Great* principles, according to Chuck Wexler, Mary Ann Wycoff, and Craig Fischer, coauthors of a report on the application of business management principles to the public sector. They quote Jody Leleck, former principal of a failing elementary school who took her school "from dreadful to very good" with the help of Collins's book. As Leleck said of the school after the transformation, "The flywheel remains in motion," a reference to Collins's metaphor of a big, heavy wheel that everyone in an organization must turn a little at a time every day, slowly at first but always in the same direction, so that momentum for change can accumulate and greatness can become a possibility.

The British firm Agilier's review concurs with all these assessments, and the reviewer marvels that the same principles and practices Collins claims to have found in eleven good-to-great companies "can be transferred to one's own life and aspirations"—a self-improvement project that might appear to be inviting a "Kumbaya" moment on a worldwide scale, until the book's charred spine turns up in the campfire of its detractors.

The Downside

Rob May, in his *Business Pundit* jeremiad, says what finally drove him to write about *Good to Great* was the fact that he had grown "sick and tired of people taking it as gospel . . . that, and the fact that the sales seem to be driven as much by churches as by businesspeople," which for May means that a major reason for the book's phenomenal success is that it has enjoyed a secondary market not typically accessible to business books. May also faults the book for its "vague but appealing BS," such as Collins's "first who, then what" formula for staffing an organization, which "basically means 'hire good people,' " according to May, who adds, "I'm willing to bet no one read the book and said 'Eureka! I've been hiring slimy weasels when I should have been hiring top performers. That is why we aren't a great company.' " May goes on to ask, "How can you definitely say whether or not a company is following the good-to-great principles?" The answer: "You can't," because "when you are looking for something specific, it is amazingly easy to find data to support your preconceptions." Thus May points to what he sees as the research's confirmation bias, a criticism that echoes Hass's passing mention of selection bias in Collins's research.

Comments along these lines are even more pointed in a pair of articles that appeared in the November 2008 issue of the Academy of Management journal *Perspectives,* with Bruce G. Resnick and Timothy L. Smunt concluding that Collins did not actually find eleven great companies, as defined by his own parameters of greatness, and that such greatness is not sustainable in any case, a judgment seconded by Bruce Niendorf and Kristine Beck, who argue that "two fatal errors" in Collins's methodology prevent *Good to Great* from offering any real evidence that the principles the book espouses, if applied to other firms over different time periods, would lead to anything other than average performance. On that score, Steven D. Levitt, writing for the Freakonomics website, takes a swipe not just at *Good to Great* but at the genre to which it belongs: "The implicit message of these business books is that the principles that these companies use not only have made them good in the past, but position them for continued success. To the extent that this doesn't actually turn out to be true, it calls into question the basic premise of these books, doesn't it?"

Other critics—notably Matthew Anderson, Russ Pierson, and an anonymous reviewer for the website of the Wharton School at the University of Pennsylvania—don't stop at charging Collins with shoddy research methodology. They also point to what they consider an even more egregious problem: Collins's original choice of a company's performance in the stock market as the measure of its greatness. According to these writers, the issue is not just that so many of Collins's "great" companies have gone out of business—and some even down in flames—since the publication of

Good to Great. It's also that, as Russ Pierson observes on his self-named website, "it doesn't take an Enron" to understand that organizational leaders at any time may be "sacrificing the long-term health of their companies for the compensation that executives gain with high performance in the short term."

SYNOPSIS

In nine chapters, Jim Collins lays out the results of five years of management research, which included studies of corporate data, interviews with corporate CEOs and managers, and analysis of individual trends and tendencies in more than a hundred major corporations. Collins eventually focused on eleven of those organizations, and *Good to Great* describes the set of principles that every one of these very good companies embraced in making the leap to greatness.

Chapter 1 explains how these eleven companies were chosen for close study. The chapter also reports Collins's finding that a culture of discipline was probably the most important determinant of each company's ability to achieve greatness.

Chapter 2 offers descriptions of Level 5 leadership and Level 5 leaders, both characterized by an unusual pairing of personal humility with fierce ambition on behalf of the company.

Chapter 3 is where Collins discusses the importance of getting the right people in the right jobs even before the company's mission and strategies are in place. By adhering to the practices described in this chapter, Collins says, companies will save time and resources in the long run.

Chapter 4 introduces the Stockdale Paradox, named for Vice Admiral James Stockdale's ability both to face the brutal facts of his situation and to maintain hope during his eight-year confinement in a Vietnamese prison camp. Collins says the same double-edged ability was essential to all the companies that made the leap to greatness.

Chapter 5 is all about the Hedgehog Concept, named for a maxim attributed to the ancient Greek poet Archilochus and later popularized by the philosopher and essayist Isaiah Berlin, which is often used to characterize the difference between generalists ("foxes," said to know "many things") and specialists ("hedgehogs," said to know "one big thing"). Collins says that a good-to-great company has to become, in effect, a specialist—a hedgehog—by discovering its Hedgehog Concept, the particular frame of reference that defines everything the company does. In the course of their research, Collins and his colleagues found that a good-to-great company took about four years, on average, to define its Hedgehog Concept, usually in a gradual, iterative way, and that once the concept had been defined, it was necessary for the company to develop a culture of discipline in order to support the concept.

Chapter 6 takes a closer look at what a culture of discipline means in action. A culture of discipline is not an authoritarian climate, Collins says. It's one in which employees are made aware of clear constraints but are also given both freedom and responsibility as they act in extremely consistent alignment with the company's Hedgehog Concept.

Chapter 7 describes the role of technology in the movement from good to great. Collins says that the good-to-great companies he studied did not adopt any technology for its own sake but carefully matched technology to their Hedgehog Concepts.

Chapter 8 introduces the metaphors of the flywheel and the doom loop. Both have to do with how the company's actions are aligned—or misaligned—with the imperatives represented by its Hedgehog Concept.

Chapter 9 briefly revisits Collins's previous book, *Built to Last,* and explains that *Good to Great* should not be seen as a sequel but as a prequel to that book. *Good to Great* shows what a company must do to achieve sustainable greatness, Collins says, whereas *Built to Last* describes what it takes for the company to attain longevity.

Key Concepts of
Good to Great

According to Jim Collins, the journey begins with **assembling the right team,** an indispensable prerequisite of **overcoming adversity** on the way to **achieving and sustaining greatness.**

I. ASSEMBLING THE RIGHT TEAM

Jim Collins believes that the move from good to great begins with assembling the right team. This is an effort that has to start at the top, Collins says—and that means the presence of what he calls **Level 5 leadership,** a term reflecting his belief that executive capability can be characterized in terms of a five-level hierarchy. At Level 1 are very capable people who have the skills needed to get their jobs done. People at Level 2 have those skills plus the ability to contribute to team-based efforts. People at Level 3, with their ability to organize teams and meet established goals, add managerial skills into the mix. Level 4 is the domain of leaders who have the ability to inspire and motivate others. And at Level 5 are very ambitious leaders who, unlike the stereotypical "rock star" CEO, combine personal humility with intense devotion to the success of the enterprise—people who tend to credit others with success and have an even stronger tendency to take primary responsibility when things go wrong. Collins believes that many people can learn to become Level 5 leaders, and that most Level 5 leaders are not brought in from outside but tend to emerge from within their companies.

Collins has some counterintuitive ideas about the qualities that team members should possess. In hiring people, he says, the important thing is not so much to look for particular skills or degrees as to look for people who already demonstrate qualities that cannot be taught—integrity, character, and a strong work ethic. In other words, he says, team members should be people who could easily become Level 5 leaders themselves. Collins also stresses that the team should be assembled even before the company's strategies are developed. If the company's vision, mission, and strategies come from the people who compose the team, he reasons, then these are the very people who will be in the best position to change course as the market or circumstances demand, and to deal successfully with the varieties of adversity that can appear during the journey from good to great.

Examples from Good to Great

- Jim Collins recounts the story of the Eckerd Corporation to illustrate the importance of assembling a strong team composed of people who are willing to challenge one another and question common assumptions about leadership and the marketplace. Jack Eckerd, son of the company's founder, used what Collins calls the "genius with a thousand helpers" model of leadership, in which a management team answers to a single powerful leader. Eckerd led his company to stellar and relatively quick success by growing two tiny drugstores in Delaware into a chain of more than a thousand stores with a large market share in the Southeast. But when Eckerd left the company to enter politics, the chain slowly but surely came undone, and there was no strong leadership team in place to guide the company into the future.

- Collins describes how Alan Wurtzel took over as CEO of his father's struggling company, which consisted of an unfocused collection of stores, all called Wards, that variously sold hi-fi equipment and assorted appliances. The new CEO surprised everyone by coming on board not with answers but with a series of questions. First he installed a carefully selected management team. Then he opened the floor to a series of debates, often launched by questions from Wurztel himself. In a situation calling for action, Wurztel acted only after having formed a sense of the situation's objective reality. He also had his own approach to staffing. If someone wasn't performing well in a particular job, he would try moving that person into another job, and sometimes into a third position, to discover whether the employee might thrive in a different role. Using the Socratic technique of questioning everything, and taking a careful, generous approach to personnel, Wurztel and his team led the company—eventually called Circuit City—to a level of greatness that it sustained for almost thirty years.

Applying the Concept

- **Are you a small-business owner?** You can take your business from good to great. Hire only people who share your most important values. Develop an overarching frame of reference that defines your core business—something you can do better than anyone else, something that drives your company economically, something you're passionate about. Stop doing anything and everything that is unrelated to your core business. And make sure you're using technology in the service of your core business, never for its own sake.

- **Are you an entry-level employee of a large organization?** Show up every day and direct all your energy and efforts toward daily progress on gains and goals encompassed by your organization's core business.

- **Are you a midlevel executive climbing the ranks?** Be ready to share your ideas honestly, and be willing to debate with others at and above your rank. But when the debates end and leaders reach a decision, make sure you're moving in the same direction as everyone else.

II. OVERCOMING ADVERSITY

According to Jim Collins, a company that wants to make the leap from good to great needs to believe in its ultimate success while also maintaining honesty and objectivity about its current performance. He illustrates this idea with the story of Vice Admiral James Stockdale, who spent eight years in a Vietnamese prison camp. Stockdale possessed two seemingly incompatible traits—the capacity to accept that he would be a prisoner for many years to come and the ability to sustain his strong belief that one day he would be set free. This capacity for maintaining a firm belief in long-term success while squarely confronting today's problems is what Collins calls **the Stockdale Paradox.**

In adverse circumstances, Collins says, a great company defines what he calls a **Hedgehog Concept:** a clear, central framework to which everything else in the company must be related and subordinated. (Collins named this concept with a famous maxim in mind—that a fox knows many things, whereas a hedgehog knows one big thing.) To define its Hedgehog Concept, a company must answer three questions: *What can we do better than any other company in the world? What drives our business economically? What are we most passionate about?* If the answers to these three questions are imagined as contiguous circles, the point where they intersect to form a common area is where the company's Hedgehog Concept will appear. This is where all the company's energy and efforts should be focused. In support of its Hedgehog Concept, the company must also compile what Collins calls a **"stop doing" list** of activities that are not aligned with the Hedgehog Concept.

In addition, Collins notes, the company's leaders must be willing to hear from their employees. For instance, the sales force tends to know what's really going on in the outside world, and members of the sales team must feel safe and even be encouraged to relay bad news to the company's leaders. Collins says that what should motivate people to act is fear of the company's reality, not fear of the company's leaders, if the company hopes to achieve and sustain greatness.

Examples from Good to Great

- In the 1970s, Walgreens stores were seen as tired throwbacks to a vanished world of small-town drugstores, complete with lunch counters. In fact, Walgreens was largely associated with its food service and even owned a chain of restaurants, Corky's, named for the company's CEO, Charles "Cork" Walgreen. But Walgreen, after much debate by the management team that he himself had put in place, concluded that the days of the company's lunch counters were numbered, and that growth in his industry had to be based on two factors—the convenience associated with Walgreens stores, and the stores' locations. Addressing these two factors became the company's Hedgehog Concept. As a result, Walgreens closed its lunch counters and purchased prominent corner lots, to make its stores more visible to and convenient for customers. Decades later, the company made a careful entry into the world of the Internet, slowly assessing where it could best serve its customers and finally developing a sophisticated online presence that customers today find useful and convenient.

- In the late 1960s, Procter and Gamble launched a consumer paper business, eclipsing Scott Paper, which had been the leader in that market but soon resigned itself to second-place status. A few years later, Darwin E. Smith, CEO of Kimberly-Clark, perceived that his company was destined for mediocrity in its core business—coated paper—and resolved to challenge both Scott Paper and Procter and Gamble in the consumer paper sector. Smith's move was ridiculed in the financial press, and the company's stock price took a hit, but Kimberly-Clark's employees were inspired. As the company's managers later explained, Procter and Gamble was such a well-run company, and there was so much respect for what that company had done, people at Kimberly-Clark got excited about rising to the challenge. They were especially proud when they beat the larger company's sales figures.

Applying the Concept

- **What does the Stockdale Paradox have to do with your checkbook?** If you're having financial trouble, you'll only block your path to resolution if you put off the tough decisions you need to make and refuse to face the facts of your situation. Things may remain difficult for a while, but you need to see your reality as it is—*and* never lose faith that eventually your problems will be in the past.

- **Is your small business *too* small?** Maybe that's because you haven't yet discovered what your core business is. If that's the case, define your company's Hedgehog Concept by asking yourself what your company can do better than any other, what drives your company economically, and what you're passionate about. Then note what your answers to those questions have in common, and turn all your energy and activity to that central commonality.

- **Is the competition breathing down your neck?** If a competitor is threatening your company's core business, consider the threat a call to arms. Learn about your competitor. How does that company operate? What are its strategies? Where does it put its resources? What are its marketing priorities? This is also the time to take a long, hard look at your own company and determine whether you're the best in the world at what you're doing. If the answer is yes, then let the threat of competition inspire you to meet the challenge head-on. If the answer is no, then keep asking yourself what you can do better than anyone else, what drives your business economically, and what you're passionate about, until you've formulated a Hedgehog Concept for your company.

III. ACHIEVING AND SUSTAINING GREATNESS

With leaders and teams in place, the company's reality objectively assessed, debates engaged and resolved, a vision formulated, and strategies determined, it's time, says Jim Collins, for the other elements of greatness to come into play. One such element is the proper use of technology. Collins warns that technology can actually block the path to success if a company relies too much on bells and whistles that serve only to funnel energy away from the company's Hedgehog Concept. According to Collins, a company that goes from good to great is one that first determines which technologies are appropriate to its Hedgehog Concept and then learns to use them in unique and innovative ways. Collins discovered that good-to-great companies have found ways to use technology as a means of accelerating their momentum, whereas other companies tend to approach technology in a less organized way, because they're afraid of being left behind if they don't try out every new technology, regardless of whether it's a good fit with the Hedgehog Concept.

Another finding of Collins's research is that none of the good-to-great companies reached greatness quickly as a result of circumstances, luck, or timing. In his view, good companies achieved greatness deliberately, in spite of market conditions and other extrinsic factors. They did it, Collins says, through disciplined focus every day. To explain this idea, Collins uses the metaphor of a **flywheel.** A flywheel revolves as part of a larger piece of machinery. The flywheel has some weight, which provides enough inertia for it to regulate the machinery's speed. In the same way, when leaders and team members focus exclusively on the company's Hedgehog Concept and push the company in the same direction on a daily basis, they turn the wheel a little at a time every day. Eventually the wheel begins to move a bit faster, and momentum gathers until finally **breakthrough** is achieved and the company reaches greatness. What that takes is patient, focused effort on the part of everyone in the company. If a leader suddenly decides to change direction and turn the flywheel the other way, the built-up momentum is lost. In addition, Collins says, as applied discipline turns the flywheel a little faster every day, employees feel more and more motivated as they watch the flywheel's speed gradually accelerate. This movement creates momentum among the employees, too, as well as a sense that great things can be achieved if they just keep turning the wheel.

Examples from Good to Great

- Perhaps a classic example of the flywheel effect occurred at Wal-Mart, which began in 1945 as a single five-and-dime. Sam Walton slowly turned the flywheel a day at a time, focusing on the Hedgehog Concept of being a discount store first for the rural South and then for other parts of the country, and he raised the number of his stores to thirty-eight in the 1960s. Between 1970 and 2000 he brought his company to the breakthrough point, opening more than three thousand stores across the country. Today Wal-Mart is the largest retail operation in the world, with annual revenues of more than $150 billion. But that achievement took more than forty years, not to mention single-minded devotion to the company's Hedgehog Concept and rigorous discipline on the part of the company's leaders, managers, and employees.

- Another element that often comes into play in great companies is a **core ideology**—a reason, beyond the profit motive, for the company to exist. For example, Walt Disney espoused the core value of providing a magical experience for his audience, particularly children. Disney began his career in 1923 as a young animator from Kansas City seeking his fortune in Los Angeles. Forced to go into business for himself, he slowly turned the flywheel by producing short animated features. Fourteen years later, Disney had accumulated enough momentum to achieve his first breakthrough—the premiere of *Snow White,* the first full-length animated feature. Disney managed to push that success to greater heights when he opened the first of a series of theme parks, an accomplishment followed by the launching of his enormously popular

TV show. Through all these enterprises, Disney maintained his core value, one so ingrained in the company that it endures today, decades after Disney's death.

Applying the Concept

- **Are you seeking greatness in your personal life and relationships?** According to Jim Collins, achieving greatness in business is never a question of mere circumstances or luck, and it seems reasonable to suppose that this is true in other areas, too. In important relationships, for example, if you're willing to show up every day and apply focus and discipline to turning the flywheel, you should be able to accumulate momentum and move toward what counts as a breakthrough in this part of your life.

- **Are you seeking greatness in your small business?** A small business can be tempted to look to technology for an easy breakthrough. As in a large company, however, technology that is not carefully aligned with the Hedgehog Concept will be nothing more than a distraction at best. But a small business can offer the kind of customer service that is difficult for a large company to deliver, and this is exactly the sort of push against the flywheel that can lead to a breakthrough and greatness for a small business.

- **Are you seeking greatness for your large organization?** A big company seeking greatness has to think the way a small business does, focusing on its Hedgehog Concept and moving the flywheel one day at a time. It can seem counterintuitive for a big company to practice the kind of patience needed for the shift to greatness. But the breakthrough will come if the company adheres to its core values and moves the flywheel a little faster, one day at a time.

Key Takeaways

- According to Jim Collins, humility and fierce determination in a company's leader, and such traits as integrity and a strong work ethic in the company's employees, are much more important than the kinds of skills that can be taught. Collins believes that the right people should be put in place even before the company's vision, mission, or strategies are determined.

- No company can withstand adversity, Collins says, unless it is able to confront the reality of its situation while also maintaining faith in its ultimate greatness. Collins believes that a company must develop a core purpose that determines every aspect of the company's efforts, and that everyone in the company must work steadily, one day at a time, toward the realization of that purpose.

- Achieving and sustaining greatness will always depend on discipline and focus, according to Collins, never on circumstances and luck. Collins says that in companies that achieve the breakthrough to greatness, that attribute is sustained by core values that transcend making a profit.

A Final Word

In *Good to Great,* Jim Collins describes the key principles and practices adopted by eleven major American corporations that he sees as having made the leap to greatness. Each of these corporations, he says, began as a moderately successful company with no particular area of distinction, but then used the same principles to achieve a level of market dominance that was sustained for at least fifteen years.

Good to Great is one of the best-selling management books of all time because it maps out specific pathways to greatness that are based on extensive research. Many of the book's recommendations—focus on what your company does better than any other, hire people of high integrity and character, work patiently every day toward your goal—seem to be little more than obvious, time-honored precepts of good business (although the book's phenomenal success may have something to say about the number of people who are still in need of such advice).

But the book also reaches some fairly counterintuitive conclusions. To take one example, leaders at the top of Collins's hierarchy of executive capabilities—Level 5 leaders—turn out not to be blustering, larger-than-life figures but humble people who turn their personal fervor toward the advancement of their companies. To take another, Collins says that before a company maps out its direction and strategy, it should put the right people in the right jobs and then let them set the company's direction. As for Collins's suggestion that a company in search of greatness find some reason beyond the profit motive for staying in business—any reason—it's a proposal that some readers see as turning the book toward a moral truth whose implications transcend the world of business.

This review has provided information about and insights into Jim Collins's *Good to Great*. The best way to continue learning about what it takes for a company to make the leap to greatness is to get a copy of the book and see how Collins's research and recommendations stack up against your own experience.

Key Terms

breakthrough the point at which a company begins to outperform its competition. The breakthrough point is reached after the company has achieved a certain level of momentum, thanks to the slow, disciplined actions of leaders and team members who are focused on the company's **Hedgehog Concept** and have been moving the **flywheel** in the same direction on a daily basis.

core ideology a company's central values, as embodied in its expressed intentions above and beyond making money. Jim Collins has found that as long as a company believes in something beyond the profit motive, it doesn't matter what that something is. The belief alone is what tends to sustain greatness, he says, and it becomes the foundation of long-term success.

culture of discipline a company climate in which people's actions are, in Jim Collins's phrase, "fanatically consistent" with the company's **Hedgehog Concept.** Collins notes that it's important not to confuse a culture of discipline with a disciplinarian culture of tyranny. When a company has a consistent system with clear constraints, Collins says, employees who are already self-disciplined, and who therefore do not need to be managed, can be given both freedom to act and ultimate responsibility for their actions. In a culture of discipline, leaders can manage the company's system instead of managing the company's employees.

doom loop Jim Collins's term for the pattern that results from a sudden change in a company's direction or a sudden shift in its goals. Sudden changes and shifts like these are often implemented by leaders who lack focus, or who become reactive to perceived changes in the marketplace. The reality represented by the doom loop is the opposite of that represented by the **flywheel.**

first who, then what   a phrase expressing the idea that *who* people are will matter more than *what* they do. Jim Collins thought at first that leaders in the good-to-great companies had set vision and strategy before turning their attention to hiring. But what he found instead was that, as he says, these leaders had put the right people on the bus, taken the wrong people off, and put the right people in the right seats before deciding where the bus would go. What this shows, Collins says, is that the old saying about people being a company's most important asset is not quite true. The whole truth, he says, is that the *right* people are a company's most important asset.

flywheel   the metaphor Jim Collins uses to capture the process of a company's movement from being good to becoming great. A flywheel is a heavy wheel that revolves in tandem with a piece of machinery, and the wheel's inertia serves to oppose and moderate fluctuations in the machinery's speed. According to Collins, that dynamic also applies to what happens when the right leader and the right team members focus on the company's **Hedgehog Concept** and unite their efforts, day by day, to push the company in the same direction. At first the flywheel moves slowly, but over time—possibly a lot of time—the flywheel gathers speed, and eventually the company reaches the **breakthrough** point.

Hedgehog Concept   the frame of reference to which everything—every strategy, idea, activity, goal, and effort—must be related and subordinated in order for a company to move from being good to becoming great. This concept takes its name from the famous maxim that compares the fox, said to know many things, to the hedgehog, said to know one big thing. The answers to three questions determine what the company's Hedgehog Concept will be: *What is the one thing we do better than anyone else in the world? What drives our economic engine? What are we most passionate about?* When these three questions are represented as contiguous circles, the point where all three circles intersect to form a common area is the point where the company's Hedgehog Concept will emerge, if there is deep understanding about that intersection.

Level 5 leaders people at the top level of the hierarchy of executive capabilities established by Jim Collins during the research that went into the writing of *Good to Great*. At the first level are leaders who are capable and competent. At the second level, leaders know how to work well with their teams. The third level is the domain of leaders who are good managers of people and goals. Leaders at the fourth level know how to use vision and inspiration to direct a group toward a clear goal. Level 5 leaders are personally humble, rarely taking credit for successes but always taking ownership when things go wrong, and relentless in the quest to guide their companies to greatness.

the Stockdale Paradox the apparently contradictory imperative of having faith in the company's ultimate success *and* not confusing that faith with the discipline required to see reality as it is and confront problems and challenges head-on. Collins named this paradox for Vice Admiral James Stockdale, a 1992 vice presidential candidate and the highest-ranking U.S. military officer to serve time in a Vietnamese prison camp. Stockdale survived eight years of deprivation, humiliation, and torture, but many others did not. Collins says Stockdale survived because he was able to face the facts, brutal though they were. Stockdale told Collins that many of his fellow prisoners were optimists—men who, again and again, would cling to the hope of being released by a certain date but then watch that date come and go while their captivity endured. In the end, the optimists had suffered so much repeated disappointment that they lost heart, gave up, and died. But Stockdale spared himself the agony of false hope. He never wavered in his belief that he would survive the ordeal and see his family again, but he also faced the truth of his situation: that his captivity would end only when the war itself ended.

"stop doing" list   the opposite of a "to do" list. This list is a compilation of daily activities and efforts that are not furthering the **flywheel**'s turning. By carefully auditing and listing such activities and efforts, a company on the journey from being good to becoming great can discover where to marshal resources and where to stop wasting time and energy.

technology accelerators   uses of technology that support a company's **Hedgehog Concept** by increasing—not creating—momentum toward the **breakthrough** point. Jim Collins says research has not borne out the common assumption that technology in and of itself can serve as a magic gateway to success. Too many companies have found themselves on the "bleeding edge" of technology, but a company on its way to greatness takes its time, does its homework, and uses only those technologies that will move the company forward on its journey. According to Collins, when a good-to-great company does find an appropriate technology, the company often becomes a pioneer in that technology's application and uses it to turn the company's **flywheel** even faster.

Recommended Reading

In addition to Jim Collins's *Good to Great: Why Some Companies Make the Leap . . . and Others Don't* (HarperBusiness, 2001), the following books are recommended for anyone who wants to learn more about what it takes for a company to achieve excellence—and even greatness.

Marcus Buckingham and Curt Coffman, *First, Break All the Rules: What the World's Greatest Managers Do Differently* (Simon & Schuster, 1999)

According to Marcus Buckingham and Curt Coffman, the conventional wisdom is wrong: truly effective managers use employees' strengths instead of trying to remedy weaknesses, hire for talent rather than for skills, and subscribe to other radical notions that go against the accepted rules of management. Drawing examples from Fortune 500 companies, small start-ups, and other types of companies across the business spectrum, the authors outline the approaches that effective managers take in motivating employees.

Jim Collins, *Good to Great and the Social Sectors: A Monograph to Accompany Good to Great* (HarperCollins, 2005)

How can a nonprofit company take the principles outlined in *Good to Great* and put them to use in a climate that is not driven by the profit motive? Jim Collins shows that nonprofits can benefit from some of the same basic tools—leadership, integrity, patience, and adherence to a specific concept—that promote success in for-profit companies.

Jim Collins and Morten T. Hansen, *Great by Choice: Uncertainty, Chaos, and Luck—Why Some Thrive Despite Them All* (HarperBusiness, 2011)
Why do some companies succeed in an environment of uncertainty while others fail? Jim Collins and Morten T. Hansen reveal the results of a nine-year investigation into this question, and they outline a number of principles for achieving success in an unpredictable world.

Jim Collins and Jerry I. Porras, *Built to Last: Successful Habits of Visionary Companies* (HarperBusiness, 2004)
3M, Wal-Mart, Disney, Hewlett-Packard, General Electric—these icons of American enterprise have lasted for many years, consistently outperforming their competitors. In this book, the product of six years of research, Jim Collins and his coauthor take a forensic look at the anatomy of these companies' success.

Steven R. Covey, *The 7 Habits of Highly Effective People: Powerful Lessons in Personal Change*, Revised Edition (Free Press, 2004)
Steven R. Covey's classic, originally published in 1990, outlines a new way both to perceive the world and to change patterns of interacting with it. The trick, as Covey shows, is learning to act from a stance of initiative instead of staying mired in a stance of reactivity.

Patrick Lencioni, *The Five Dysfunctions of a Team: A Leadership Fable* (Jossey-Bass, 2002)
Using a fable about a CEO and a leadership crisis she faces, Patrick Lencioni describes five common hurdles that confront even the most successful teams. The author suggests steps for overcoming those hurdles and outlines solutions intended to help teams solve common problems and forge ahead to success.

Thomas J. Peters and Robert H. Waterman Jr., *In Search of Excellence: Lessons from America's Best-Run Companies* (HarperBusiness, 2004)
In this celebrated study of forty-three of America's best-run companies, Peters and Waterman describe what they regard as the eight attributes of a successful company.

Bibliography

Matthew Anderson, "A Peer Review of 'Good to Great' by Jim Collins"
The Social Medicine Portal, February 16, 2009 (accessed March 9, 2013)
http://www.socialmedicine.org/2009/02/16/critical-social-medicine/a-peer-review-
of-good-to-great-by-jim-collins

Mike Bonem, "Good to Great to Godly"
Leadership Journal, Winter 2010 (accessed March 14, 2013)
http://www.christianitytoday.com/le/2010/winter/goodgreatgodly.html?start=1

"Book Review: 'Good to Great' by Jim Collins"
Agilier, undated (accessed March 10, 2013)
http://www.agilier.com/book-reviews/good-to-great.html

"*Good to Great* Falls Short of Its Title"
Knowledge@Wharton, December 19, 2001 (accessed March 9, 2013)
http://knowledge.wharton.upenn.edu/special_sections/121901_ss5.html

William J. Hass, "Book Review: Transforming Bad to Good and Good to Great"
Turnaround, January 31, 2003 (accessed March 9, 2013)
http://www.turnaround.org/Publications/Articles.aspx?objectID=1623

Jeff Janssen, "How to Go from a Good to a Great Team"
Championship Coaches Network, undated (accessed March 14, 2013)
http://www.championshipcoachesnetwork.com/public/292.cfm

Steven D. Levitt, "From Good to Great ... to Below Average"
Freakonomics, July 28, 2008 (accessed March 9, 2013)
http://www.freakonomics.com/2008/07/28/from-good-to-great-to-below-average

Kevin Maney, "True Believers Ignite Super Sales Rate for 'Good to Great' "

USA Today, May 18, 2004 (Accessed March 17, 2013)

http://usatoday30.usatoday.com/money/books/2004-05-18-good-to-great_x.htm

Rob May, "Why 'Good to Great' Isn't Very Good"

Business Pundit, January 31, 2006 (accessed March 9, 2013)

http://www.businesspundit.com/why-good-to-great-isnt-very-good

Bruce Niendorf and Kristine Beck, "*Good to Great,* or Just Good?"

Perspectives, November 2008, 13–20 (Accessed March 17, 2013)

http://www.business.unr.edu/faculty/simmonsb/badm720/ampgoodtogreat2.pdf

Russ Pierson, "Bad to Worst: A Review of *Good to Great*"

Russ Pierson, undated (accessed March 9, 2013)

http://blog.russpierson.com/bad-to-worst-a-review-of-good-to-great-dmingm-61301

Bruce G. Resnick and Timothy L. Smunt, "From Good to Great to … "

Perspectives, November 2008, 6–12 (Accessed March 17, 2013)

http://kimboal.ba.ttu.edu/Readings%202008/Rensnick%20and%20Smunt2008.pdf

Chuck Wexler, Mary Ann Wycoff, and Craig Fischer, "*Good to Great*" *Policing: Application of Business Management Principles in the Public Sector*

Community Oriented Policing Services (COPS), U.S. Department of Justice / Police Executive Research Forum (PERF), 2007 (Accessed March 17, 2013)

http://cops.usdoj.gov/files/RIC/Publications/good_to_great.pdf

CPSIA information can be obtained at www.ICGtesting.com
Printed in the USA
LVOW131357030713

341294LV00001B/42/P